Word Soup

Sunil Singh

 pencil

ISBN 978-93-5667-131-7
© Sunil Singh 2022
Published in India 2022 by Pencil

A brand of

One Point Six Technologies Pvt. Ltd.
123, Building J2, Shram Seva Premises,
Wadala Truck Terminal, Wadala (E)
Mumbai 400037, Maharashtra, INDIA
E connect@thepencilapp.com
W www.thepencilapp.com

DISCLAIMER: *The opinions expressed in this book are those of the authors and do not purport to reflect the views of the Publisher.*

Author biography

Sunil Singh is the author of two other books, this being his third book . Ghubar & Other poems (2020), WORDS (2022). He lives in Mumbai . His last stint was with an International Property Consultancy headquartered at Chicago, Illinois, United States. You can email him at sunil.s@writeme.com. You can follow him on twitter @sunil24by7 , Instagram & Facebook on @2go2sunil.

CONTENTS

Sometimes

Sometimes I feel insignificant
as superfluous as an extra a in laager
especially when I am
living like a hermit crab in a borrowed shell
sometimes I get so swelled up by the rude behaviours of
others
and do not want to say the phrase
yet somehow by the cruel checkmate logic of conversation
is compelled to say :
thank you
we lived together for half a decade
and we went from knowing each other to staying with a
stranger
and then when we parted ways
it felt like I understood you
like a last day in a foreign country
you finally figure out where to get a good coffee
or drinks from
but then you have to leave
and you won't ever be back
Or sometimes it's like meeting old people
who are either bald or has grey hair
I would never know what colour their hair used to be

Digital sabbath

Wish there would be 9 days in a week
so i could keep 2 days for the digital sabbath
the days when I would live like a primitive being
no emails , phones or web at all
just long runs on the beaches
with mornings that are
quite and mellow
and devoid of stimuli from an external data
and twilight around the campfire with loved ones
consuming stories and food and drinks and comfort

World today

Ukraine bleeding
Myanmar bleeding
Sri Lanka burning
how long do we go on
pretending and thanking god it's not us
the poison that's spoils the river
spoils the ocean too

Strange animal

Human is a strange animal
He wants what he doesn't have
And doesn't want what he has
Only to realise later that he really wants what he had but
thought he doesn't want it when he had it

Others plate

People who look at others plate
Are perpetually busy looking at others plate
People who focus on their plate
Are perpetually busy looking at their own plate
Winners are busy focusing on their goals
Losers are busy focusing on winners

What people want

Not secularism
not fundamentalism
not liberalism
all people want is a dignified life
with a spurring economy
and peace of mind

Divide and rule

Till the time the news
on the tv screen is split in three parts
my country will continue being divided and ruled

Slavery

You know what is slavery
it's knowing your freedom
and still not having guts to follow it
It's knowing where love is
Still being afraid to love
Its knowing what living is
Still surviving and not not living
It's wishing for a life of your dreams
And Having no guts to create one
And wishing you were dead
And reborn in a perfect situation
To start again

Meanings

We were siting on the edge of a cliff
immersed in the beauty of the sunrise
the green sheet of jungle flowing below our feet dangling
to unfathomable depths like love
the clouds moving in front of us like a table where the
whole beauty was being served to us
And then we realised how terrifying it is to
be at the edge
the fear sent shivers in our spines
And we left the scary cliff
there was no beautiful sunrise
the unfathomable depths were eerie without love

Phoenix

The past is the ashes
the future is the new tree
the magic is to use the past as a manure to grow the future
like a phoenix rising from its ashes
staring fresh unsoiled by the catastrophes of its world

Plan

While walking on the beach
to avoid my shoes from getting wet
i judge the waves
knowing for sure the next one will be a little larger than the
last one
however , there comes a huge one that washes my plan to
keep the shoes dry

Club

A place where everyone is happy to
find other people from the identical social strata
where everyone exchange pleasantries, laughing out their
lungs
and completely at ease

Evening

It's been a tardy day
evening sunsets are beautiful
sometimes more than sunrises
peaceful and stoical
like a fresh hour
played some jazz in the background
made some tea
lit incense sticks
and combed through the books
like a drowning man clutch at a straw to set the tone for
the evening
starting to read a new book is like an abyss that
encapsulates and metamorphosis me

Words

The night was dark like a coffee sans milk
In the silhouettes of its hot steam
I tasted the rancid and bitter words
And heard you sing the songs of springs
Your fragrance lingers like a sweet vodka breath
I remember you in your words
The words uttered
And the words unuttered

Book

A Book is an abyss
that encapsulates
and metamorphosis
the stories devoured
devours back
the dopamine released
from the self inflicted wounds
is sheer masochism
worth a trek
Journey where one bleeds
and gets healed
Power
Peace of mind
Purpose
Understanding
Light
laughter and love

Surrender

I surrender to you
Let me vanish into you
Like smoke losing itself in the air
Let me disappear into you
From the clutches of shadows and light

Journey

Imagine a train journey
that's exactly what life is
Enjoy the weather peeking out of the window
get down at different stations to stretch and have some
chai
Talk to strangers
Share stories
Eat with them

Father

You left
I can't believe that I will never see you again
I was afraid of loosing you
now you aren't there
sleep well
Wish you peace of mind
wherever you are
I love you Pappa
God speed

Funeral

All broken souls supporting each other
Realising the fact how short life is
All the bragging ,ego ,selfishness , goals, aims and dreams
are stories and so transient
Ultimately the soul leaves
The body is turned to ashes
The bones are submerged in the river Ganga
All the broken souls
Still eating out each other
Trying to fill their bellies with others meat
Till they die
Till it's their funeral

Love

Older than the pyramids
Older than the Stonehenge
Older than the primitive cave paintings
Love is the only thing
That we need to know
It's the ocean that engulfs
All that is to known and needs to be known
Love is the only knowledge

Hero

To protect and to serve
With a desire to be loved and understood
To survive
To succeed
To be free
To express
To revenge
And right wrongs

Mentor

Someone who could motivate
Inspire
Guide
Train
Provide gifts for the journey
Who knows the ropes
Has a road map to unknown country
Can help with knowledge at the right juncture
However mentors are earned
By being kind
Sharing food with them
Protecting them
Being a well wisher

Obstacles

The obstacles aren't to stop us
From growth and progress
But to test to see
If we are really resolved to change
If we don't get putt off by outward appearance of the obstacles
And see past the outward impression to the skin deep realty
The obstacles are actually welcoming us
They aren't threatening enemies but
Useful allies
Indicating that new power and success is coming
It helps us to discover resistance as a source of strength
As in bodybuilding
Greater the resistance greater the strength
As in martial arts the opponents strength can be used against them
To eventually feel compassion for the enemies and transcend rather than destroy them
Ways to deal with obstacle are umpteen
To turn around and run
To attack head on
To deceit craft fully to get by
Bribe or appease

To make ally or
To get into the skin of the opponent

Motivation

I handled the imbalanced life
through my own coping mechanisms and defences
and then a newness entered and shifted
the balance
Nothing was ever same anymore
Made a decision
Took an action
Faced the challenge
Something inside us knows
When we are prepared to change
and the change arrives

Shadow

Express healthy anger & grief
Affection , creativity or unexplored potential or psychic
abilities
Acknowledge the roads not taken
And Possibilties eliminated by making choices at different
stages of life
The suppressed psychic abilities
Bring them to light
Express the neglected and forgotten
There's a vulnerability in our shadows and shady people
too
A dash of goodness that is human and admirable and real
With weakness and emotions
Shadow is sometimes trying to destroy our weakness
To bring out the best in us
Explore and express the shadows head-on

Courage

We don't reveal courage
Unless we are frightened
Courage is shown
to overcompensate for our fears
There's an antiseptic quality to it
Which is clean and impersonal

Ally

Someone who could suggest an alternate path to problem-solving
Someone who could round out your personality
Who helps to bring into use the unexpressed and unused parts of the being
Someone who could guide in spiritual or emotional matters
Someone who is helpful and friendly
Someone who is wise and can hold up a mirror against the hypocrisy of society
Someone who can help cope with reality
Someone who could guide through the subtleties of love , protect and help with little extra brain power
Someone who could encourage to lead a good and useful life
Someone who could look out and keep the you on the right path
Someone who is as close as side pocket
Someone who could serve as a conscience
Someone who could see the world with fresh eyes
Someone who could view the world and society extremely differently
Someone who is talented and gifted
Someone who can be a companion, a sparring partner , conscience or comic relief

Someone who could help in errands
Carry messages
Scout locations of the road map of life
Someone convenient to talk to
To bring out human feelings
Someone who could humanise our existence
Add extra dimension to our personality
Someone who could challenge us to be more open and balanced
Someone who could bring laughter
And love
Someone who is our coping and defence mechanism to the imbalanced life
Be that someone
Be that ally

Mumbai

The earthy rains with chai
Victoria Terminus Station with swarms of cosmopolitans
The Suave and calm and composed metro train filled with dreams ,aspirations and respect for existence overlooking the slums on one side and Highrise in the other
The sea gulls flocking on marine drive and Girgaon chowpatty during January to March
The pigeons thriving alongside humans
The city of film
The queens necklace
More emotions expressed in real life than in plays performed in theatres at Prithvi and NCPA
The umpteen coffee shops brewing more dreams than the coffee
some rancid and bitter like espresso
Some sweet and soothing like hot chocolate
The Gateway of India inviting people from the country and across the world to visit long after the outside world has stopped using it as an entrance to the country
The magnificent sea link that feels like freedom and saves time and connects Bandra to Worli
The six sigma tiffin system
The Mumbai cricket club
People walking ,jogging , strolling , chatting
On the Bandra promenade and Juhu beach

The Highrise towers that are more high in prices than
than the height from the sea level
The kala ghoda art festivals
The local trains

Be in love

Be in love
It gives meaning to life
Life is much richer when you are in love

Peace of mind

All we pursue is peace of mind
Through different vehicles

Stay Love

Do not forget me after making me fall in love with you
do not disappear from my life after promising to stay

Superpower

Stay polite
Respectful
And calm
In turmoil
Storms
Disrespect or
When someone provokes or angers you

Happiness

Everyone is fighting a battle in their heads
It could be money
It could be love
It could be health
We should give happiness to the world
And not share our sadness
Our sadness is ours to keep
Like everyone has their own sadness
We can either crib and spread our sadness to others
Or we can be positive and spread happiness to others

Hypocrisy

How do you cope with a society that itself is coping with its rules and rituals by not following them under the mask of preaching and pretending that it's right and should be followed .

How do you cope with a situation where your foe has the same pain but he wishes you to bear it to prove that he fits in well while he doesn't bear it and only pretends too.

How do you wash the fear from the minds that's almost become like a second skin and rusted the brains to the level of genes

How do make a foe an ally when he s afraid and living in dilemma of right and wrong

Where your and his wrongs are the same

But to inflict the wrong on you has become his right and coping mechanism and defence system to live in society

How do live in a society that's synonymous with hypocrisy and utterly reprehensible

Opinion

Drop your opinions about everything
as we are wrong about everything anyways
strong opinions
only cause stress
There are as many opinions as there are people
how can your opinion be the right one
out of gazillions floating around
It's neither right nor wrong
It is what it is
If it spreads love it's good
If it doesn't change it

Walk

Sometimes life becomes like an empty canvass
You are the brush and and your actions paints the infinite
possibilities
Like a clean sky after storms and heavy rains
Pristine and scary
You are afraid to take a decision
But you have to take one
And walk

The drama of life

When the winds are favourable
followed by a calm before the storm
And then a catalyst predicament
That turns the tail winds to head winds
When the world seems turned upside down
Like someone has scattered your life
When you can't go back to where you came from
When you can't stay where you are
Then you make a decision
You take a road that's unchartered
You become kind for you know how it feels and help
someone
You fall in love
And You start living a new story

Solution

To discover a solution
One must see the problem first

God

when I thought I have grasped it all
he changed the game

Interfering with The Creator

I didn't have say in
Where I was born
I will not have a say in
Where will I die
But I try and have a say in
Everything that happens between my birth and death
Like a cat that wants to choose the colour of its hair
Do cats behave like that
Or maybe It's-anthropomorphism-to-control-how-a-cat-
thinks

Unconditional love

In the black and barren days and nights of life
when the lights are out and you have nothing at all
If you have just one person with an unconditional love
That's all you need to go through the hardships
and bloom miraculously

Vulnerable

Womb of existence - a place from where we are born and

where we return when we die.
And we bear a wound-of-separation from this place throughout our lives

Grey

Layered and grey is life
Been it white or black
Been it binary
Been it rose and thorns
innocence covered with naivety
selfishness covered with sweetness
care covered with curtness
greed wrapped as help
love wrapped as selflessness

Pain

Pain reminds me
of being human
It brings me home to how flawed I am
When I see the pain in the eyes of someone I love
It reminds me of my limits

Ashes to New Branches

How long does it take to rise from one's ashes
To decide and act
To take charge of life
To have the gall to start living second story
To see fear in the eye
To beat one's demons
How long does it take
To fall in love
After going through cold winters of life
How long does it take
to grow new branches
on a tree turned to ashes

Being loved

The true peace of mind

Is being loved unconditionally by someone
Every other peace of mind
Is a soul that's given up on life
tired
and beaten up
It's death

Promises

The promises we make

Are meant to be kept
To keep the love behind those promises
It's difficult at times
To trek the path
When the road is lost
The vision is blurred
When you may walk away from the summit
Intending to walk towards it
The promises
Are like love
Which needs to be kept

Doors

The doors that are closed
And not opening in lieu of knocking time and again
Stop visiting them
Look for new doors
Life is short
You might find an apt one that's not even shut

Underdogs

If the underdog doesn't win
The Stories won't be interesting

Dream

You are as rich as your dreams
It's an unfathomable ocean of possibilities
Agreed we have a finite life with invite resources
But we have a super powerful mind
Which can enter anything and
Escape from anything
Why ask for what others have
When you can choose to have anything from the abundance
Why just crawl from moment to moment
When you can really fly through the life
Dream !
For you are only as rich as your dreams

Gold out of straw

How do you make
Gold out of straw
There's sadness , pain & frustration
How do you use it to make something beautiful
How do you bounce back
When all seems to be lost
How do you smile
When being happy feels guilty

Composition

When noise is organised using wisdom
It becomes music
When chaos is organised using wisdom
It becomes life
When words are organised using love , soul and wisdom
It becomes a poem